Morning by Morning

A Quiet Time Guide for Beginners

Josie Quimba Sinclair

ISBN-13: 978-1500700928

Cover photography and design: Kerry Sinclair

I lovingly dedicate this book to my parents, Jose Tingzon and Claudia Perez Tingzon, who are now with the Lord. Their love for God's Word and encouragement to do my daily "devotions" impacted me at a young age, and their early morning times spent with the Lord planted the first seeds of "Quiet Time" in my heart.

Table of Contents

Preface

Welcome to the family of God! When you took that step of faith to receive Jesus Christ into your life as your Savior and Lord, the Bible says you became a child of God (John 1:12). You were spiritually born again! You have begun a new relationship with him that will last forever. But your new life has to be nourished so that you will grow healthy and strong in your faith.

When I first made the choice to follow Jesus Christ, I did not receive the help I needed. Without enough guidance, my spiritual growth was very slow. It was only later that I began to grow closer to Jesus and understand more about him and his will for me. The thing that helped me most was learning to spend time alone with him. This is commonly called a Quiet Time.

From our conversations with international students, including those who had returned home as Christians, my husband Kerry and I saw the need for a guide to help them spend quality time with Jesus. They said they wished they could have had such a guide when they first became Christians. Some of them expressed inconsistency in their Quiet Time and said they needed help to maintain it. Others had never learned to have a Quiet Time at all. They looked forward to this simple guide—both for their own use and as a tool to help other new believers grow in their faith.

I wrote this guide with international students in mind. However, it should also help any Christian who has not formed the habit of having a daily Quiet Time.

I hope it will accomplish three things: first, help you establish a regular and consistent time alone with Jesus; second, increase your love for him and his word; and third, help you put into practice what you are learning from the Bible. By establishing this daily habit of meeting with the Lord, you should find yourself growing to be more like him.

My prayer is that Quiet Time will become a big part of your daily life—for all of your life—so that you may grow in wisdom and in favor with God and men (Luke 2:52).

Enjoy your time with the Lord Jesus!

Part 1 – Introduction to Quiet Time

WHAT is Quiet Time?

Quiet Time is a scheduled time you set aside every day to meet with Jesus alone. When you gave your life to him, a new relationship began. He not only became your Savior and Lord (master), but your friend (John 15:13)! As your friend, he wants to meet with you and spend time with you. He desires your companionship. If you have a friend, don't you want to hang out with her or him? As you do, your friendship grows. You share each other's secrets. You begin to like the same things, and even know each other's thoughts! In the same way, as you spend more time with Jesus, reading his word and talking to him in prayer, you get to know him better and your relationship with him grows deep and strong. You begin to know what pleases him. When you spend time with the Lord, you are spiritually nurtured; you experience his close friendship and his great love and care for you.

The most important habit I developed as a new Christian was to spend time alone with the Lord. I make sure I schedule time each day to read God's word, think about it, listen to him, write down what I'm hearing from him, talk with him, sing to him, worship him, or just quietly wait on him.

WHY have a Quiet Time?

Because Jesus left us an example! Mark 1:35 says, *"Very early in the morning, while it was still dark, Jesus got up, left the house and went off to a solitary place, where he prayed"* (NIV). In fact, when his disciples were too busy, he urged them to *"come with me by yourselves to a quiet place"* to be with him (Mark 6:31, NIV). If Jesus spent time alone with his Heavenly Father, shouldn't you and I do the same?

WHEN should I have my Quiet Time?

"I rise early, before the sun is up; I cry out for help and put my hope in your words. I stay awake through the night, thinking about your promise." (Psalm 119:147-148)

"Be ready in the morning to climb up Mount Sinai and present yourself to me on the top of the mountain." (Exodus 34:2)

There is no rule for when you should have your Quiet Time (QT). I do mine first thing in the morning because I concentrate better, it's quiet, there are fewer distractions, and members of my family are still asleep. When I was a student nurse intern and lived in the dorm, I set my alarm clock 30 minutes before our wake up time. You must decide what time of the day is best for you. If you don't have a fixed schedule, you'll probably find yourself forgetting to have these times alone with God. There are those who do their QT during lunch break in school or at work. If you are a mom with small children, you can be flexible. Do it when the kids are taking a nap during the day, or after you put them to bed at night. Some people who work during the day do their QT in the evening or before they go to bed, but most of them wake up a little early so they can spend their first moments with the Lord. The important thing is to do it regularly and consistently.

HOW LONG should a Quiet Time be?

You should talk it over with the Lord and decide. Ten minutes? Twenty? Thirty? Discipline yourself to spend that length of time as you have agreed with him. You can increase the amount of time you spend with the Lord as needed. I don't think he will mind!

Whatever time of day you set to have your QT, know that you are meeting the One who loves you more than anyone else ever can. Honor that time. There will be days when you may not "feel" the Lord's presence. Be assured he is there, because he promised *"I will be with you always"*! He wants you to draw close to him. Remember, Jesus is waiting for you!

WHERE should I have my Quiet Time?

Jesus said, *"But when you pray, go into your room, close the door and pray to your Father, who is unseen. Then your Father, who sees what is done in secret, will reward you" (*Matthew 6:6, NIV). Find a prayer place—that is, any place that works well for you to talk with God. It may be a chair by your bed, a quiet corner in the library, or your kitchen table. In fact, when I was a student nurse intern and had little privacy, one corner of our restroom was my prayer place! Wherever it is, you want it to be as quiet as possible–away from noise (like TV) and interruptions (like phone calls or text messages), or other distractions like email, social media, etc. Just turn off your phone...you will survive!

For many years now, my prayer place is the sofa in our living room. Sometimes, when the weather is nice, I go to a nearby park to have my QT. I enjoy the peace and quiet and beauty the place offers. The Bible says that on one occasion Jesus *"went up into the hills by himself to pray. Night fell while he was there alone" (*Matthew 14:23). It might not be safe for you to be outside alone (especially for women), but choose a safe place where you can meet privately with Jesus.

Perhaps you work long hours and have a long commute. Even though it's not private, your prayer place might have to be your seat on the train, subway, or bus! Or perhaps it's your work desk during lunch time. Just do the best you can with whatever situation you have.

HOW do I do it?

Once you're settled in your prayer place, the important thing to remember is that you are meeting with the Lord of the universe, someone who loves you and wants your full attention. So, "*Be still before the Lord and wait patiently for him*" (Psalm 37:7a, NIV).

There are many possible ways to have a QT with the Lord. It can be as simple as just reading your Bible and praying. However, there are many people who need some structure and guidance for how to do it. They say things like, "I don't know where to start", or "I don't know how to fill up the time".

This guide will teach you four suggested methods for doing your QT. You will learn helpful principles from these methods. However, each of us is different. As time goes on, you can adapt these principles and find your own favorite ways of spending time with the Lord.

Preparation for Quiet Time

1. Make a commitment with the Lord to meet him at a specific time each day. You could pray something like this: *Lord, I want to grow closer to you and be more like you. With your help, I will do my best to meet with you every day at ______ (time) for _____ minutes.*

If you miss your appointment with him for some reason, don't feel condemned, and don't give up on trying to establish this habit. Think of it this way: If you miss breakfast, what will you do? You'll eat a bigger lunch, or eat a snack during your break. You certainly won't say, "I'm a failure at eating breakfast, so I won't even try to eat breakfast anymore!" In the same way, a missed QT shouldn't discourage you from continuing to develop the habit. And you might still be able to find some other time that day to spend time with God.

2. Schedule your QT in your calendar or appointment book as you would any other appointment.

3. Set your alarm the night before or program it in your cell phone for a daily reminder.

4. If you plan to have your QT in the morning before work or school, go to bed early so you can get up early. Pray that God will give you victory over Satan who would like to stop you from meeting with God.

5. The night before, have the things ready that you will need for your QT. You will definitely want...
___Your Bible (whatever language you can understand best)
___This QT guide (while you're starting out)
___Pen or pencil
___A Quiet Time notebook*
___Index cards or notepad to write your memory verse

Some optional items you might want to include are...
___Dictionary (this is VERY helpful)
___Worship music (you may want to sing or listen to a worship song to help you focus on the Lord)

I have my QT materials ready in my QT tote bag the evening before, so in the morning I just grab it on the way to my prayer place.

**I strongly suggest you get a blank notebook for your QT, because you will need more space to write your thoughts, prayers, questions, and lessons learned from the Lord. Also, you can use it to write down distracting thoughts that come to your head during your QT. If you suddenly remember something that you need to do, just write a quick note to yourself: "Buy Naomi a gift", or "Call Grandmother". Then you won't have to worry that you'll forget, and you can quickly re-focus on the Lord.*

The Format for Quiet Time: PRAY'R
Now, how do you go about your Quiet Time? The acronym **PRAY'R** (**P**repare your Heart, **R**ead, **A**sk, **Y**our Plan of Action, **R**emain in Prayer) is an easy format to follow. (You will notice acronyms or abbreviations throughout this guide. When I was in nursing school, acronyms helped me remember medical terms. So I hope this will help you associate the words with a format or method.)

You start with…

♥ Prepare your Heart. Tell the Lord that you are giving him your full attention for the next however many minutes you have decided to spend time with him. You might pray something like this: *"Lord Jesus, please give me understanding as I read and think about your word. Make your truth clear to me. Help me to concentrate. As your word says, 'open my eyes that I may see wonderful things in your law'."* Included in this guide are daily

Bible verses that you can add to your prayer of preparation as you begin your Quiet Time.

📖 Read God's Word. For the first two weeks you will find the Bible readings printed for you. If you don't already own a Bible, **you will need to get one before Week 3.** See **Appendix C** for information about finding a Bible.

? Ask questions that will help you understand the passage. Your goal is not only to ask questions but to gain insights from God as you interact with the passage, and then to apply these truths to your life. The four QT methods (**ABC**, **FLY**, **PURE**, and **PICTURES**) will give you different ways of doing your Quiet Time. Every week you will be introduced to one of these methods. On the fifth week, you will be on your own; that is, you can choose one or a combination of these methods to use in your QT. These are just suggestions; there are other ways to do QT, too!

See **Appendix A** for examples of each method.

After doing the Ask segment, go to...

⇨ Your Plan of Action. James 1:22 says, *"But don't just listen to God's word. You must do what it says. Otherwise, you are only fooling yourselves."* This is an important part of your QT, so you shouldn't skip this! In the space provided for you, write down one, two, or three ways you can put into practice the lessons you just learned. Your plan should be specific and achievable. Make use of action verbs and a time frame. For example, "I will *memorize* (action verb) Romans 3:23 by the *end of the day*" (time frame); or, "I will *ask* Lin *tomorrow* to attend the Bible Study with me"; or, "I will *tell* Juan what I learned in my QT when I *meet* with him *this evening*".

Briefly review your Plan of Action at the end of the day or each week. Did you fulfill it? If you did, then put a check mark before the number to indicate you have done it. This will also remind you to do it if you haven't already.

Remain in Prayer. You should be having a conversation with the Lord through all of the PRAY'R steps, but now it's time to really focus on talking to him. I like to use what I call **DATE** praying. (Please go to **Appendix A** for a full explanation of DATE praying.) Here is a quick example of what it is:

Describe God ("Lord, you are such a loving Father! All of your ways are right and true.")
Ask forgiveness ("I was wrong to lie to my parents. Please cleanse me from this sin.")*
Thank him ("Thank you for my good health. Thank you for giving me enough food to eat.")
Express needs ("Lord, please heal my uncle from his sickness, and open his eyes to know you.")
When praying for other people it's helpful to have a prayer list. Part 3 ("My Prayer Organizer") gives you ideas to help you start one.

__A word of warning__: It's very possible that this book or your QT notebook could be read by another person. Be careful about writing anything that could be used against you or cause misunderstanding. Sometimes it will be wiser to just pray about something and not write it down, or to write it in such a way that only you know what is meant.

Part 2 - Daily Quiet Time Guide

Week 1: NEW LIFE in Christ

As soon as you made the decision to put your faith in Jesus as your Savior and Lord, you became a child of God (John 1:12). You are spiritually born again! This week's Quiet Times will focus on your **NEW LIFE** in Christ. The seven topics are Biblical truths assuring you that this new life you have in Christ is real! God's word says that you are a **N**ew Person, you have **E**ternal Life, you are a **W**ork in progress, you are **L**oved, you are **I**ndwelt by Christ, you are **F**orgiven, and you have the Holy Spirit to **E**mpower you.

The **ABC** Method

This week you will use the ABC method. This method of Quiet Time allows you to select verses that stand out to you after asking yourself three questions:

A. Which verse do I find most **A**ssuring? (Gives me peace, certainty and confidence)

B. Which verse is my most **B**eloved? (My favorite)

C. Which verse do I find most **C**onvicting? (That is, makes me aware of my sin)

After selecting your verses, ask the following questions for A, B, and C:

How would I say the verse in my own words or language?

What does this verse mean for me? How will I live and think differently because of this verse?

Read the verses you've chosen, slowly and prayerfully. Look up the meaning of unfamiliar words. You may want to write your chosen verses in your QT notebook**.** Ask the Holy Spirit to show you things in your life that he wants you to get rid of, improve on, continue with, or begin doing.

(See **Appendix A** if you'd like to see an example of how to do the ABC method.)

Day 1 I am a........**N**ew person
Day 2 I have.......**E**ternal life
Day 3 I am a........**W**ork in progress
Day 4 I am...........**L**oved
Day 5 I am...........**I**ndwelt by Christ
Day 6 I am...........**F**orgiven
Day 7 I am...........**E**mpowered by the Holy Spirit

Week 1, Day 1: I am a **N**ew person!

♥ Prepare your Heart
"Let my words and my thoughts be pleasing to you, LORD*, because you are my mighty rock and my protector."* (Psalm 19:14, CEV)

📖 Read
John 1:12 *"But to all who believed him and accepted him, he gave the right to become children of God. They are reborn—not*

with a physical birth resulting from human passion or plan, but a birth that comes from God."

2 Corinthians 5:17 *"This means that anyone who belongs to Christ has become a new person. The old life is gone; a new life has begun!"*

Galatians 2:20 *"My old self has been crucified with Christ. It is no longer I who live, but Christ lives in me. So I live in this earthly body by trusting in the Son of God, who loved me and gave himself for me."*

Ephesians 2:4,5 *"But God is so rich in mercy, and he loved us so much, that even though we were dead because of our sins, he gave us life when he raised Christ from the dead. (It is only by God's grace that you have been saved!)"*

1 Peter 1:23-24 *"For you have been born again, but not to a life that will quickly end. Your new life will last forever because it comes from the eternal, living word of God. As the Scriptures say, 'People are like grass; their beauty is like a flower in the field. The grass withers and the flower fades'".*

? **A**sk: What do I find to be...

The most **A**ssuring verse(s): ______________________

How would I say the verse in my own words or language?

What does this verse mean for me? How will I live and think differently because of this verse?

My most **B**eloved verse(s): ________________________

How would I say the verse in my own words or language?

What does this verse mean for me? How will I live and think differently because of this verse?

The most **C**onvicting verse(s): _______________

How would I say the verse in my own words or language?

What does this verse mean for me? How will I live and think differently because of this verse?

⇨ Your Plan of Action: Because of what I learned today, with the Lord's help I will...

__1. Stop doing _________________________, because I know it's part of my old life, not my new life in Christ.

__2. Share what I learned today with _______________ by (time frame) ____________

__3.

Remain in Prayer (see **Appendix A** for more explanation of DATE praying)

Describe God
Ask forgiveness
Thank him
Express needs

Week 1, Day 2: I have **E**ternal life
[*Eternal = never-ending*]

Prepare your Heart

Lord, your instructions are perfect and trustworthy; they give me life and make me wise (see Psalm 19:7). I commit my time to you now.

Read

John 3:16 *"For God loved the world so much that he gave his only Son, so that everyone who believes in him will not perish but have eternal life."*

John 3:36 *"And anyone who believes in God's Son has eternal life. Anyone who doesn't obey the Son will never experience eternal life but remains under God's angry judgment."*

1 John 5:11-13 *"And this is what God has testified: He has given us eternal life, and this life is in his Son. Whoever has the Son has life: whoever does not have God's Son does not have life. I have written this to you who believe in the name of the Son of God, so that you may know you have eternal life."*

John 10:27-30 Jesus speaking: *"My sheep listen to my voice; I know them, and they follow me. I give them eternal life, and they will never perish. No one can snatch them away from me, for my Father has given them to me, and he is more powerful than anyone else. No one can snatch them from the Father's hand. The Father and I are one."*

John 17:2-3 *"...He gives eternal life to each one you have given him. And this is the way to have eternal life—to know you, the only true God, and Jesus Christ, the one you sent to earth."*

Titus 3:4-7 *"When God our Savior revealed his kindness and love, he saved us, not because of the righteous things we had done, but because of his mercy. He washed away our sins, giving us a new birth and new life through the Holy Spirit. He generously poured out the Spirit upon us through Jesus Christ our Savior. Because of his grace he declared us righteous and gave us confidence that we will inherit eternal life."*

? **A**sk: What do I find to be...

The most **A**ssuring verse(s): ______________________

How would I say the verse in my own words or language?

What does this verse mean for me? How will I live and think differently because of this verse?

My most **B**eloved verse(s): _______________________

How would I say the verse in my own words or language?

What does this verse mean for me? How will I live and think differently because of this verse?

The most **C**onvicting verse(s): ______________

How would I say the verse in my own words or language?

What does this verse mean for me? How will I live and think differently because of this verse?

➪ **Y**our Plan of Action: Because of what I learned today, with the Lord's help I will...

__1. Memorize John 3:16 today. (It's easier to memorize when you write the verse on a card or notepad to carry with you. You can glance at it while walking, eating, or riding on the subway. Save your cards and review your memory verses on a regular basis.

__2. Share what I learned today with ____________

__3.

Remain in Prayer

Describe God

Ask forgiveness
Thank him
Express needs

Week 1, Day 3: I am a **W**ork in progress
[*Work in progress = unfinished project*]

♥ Prepare your Heart
My Lord, your commandments are right, and they bring joy to my heart. They are clear, and they show me how to live (see Psalm 19:8). Make my heart ready to receive your word.

📖 Read
Romans 12:2 *"Don't copy the behavior and customs of this world, but let God transform you into a new person by changing the way you think. Then you will learn to know God's will for you, which is good and pleasing and perfect."*

Ephesians 2:10 *"For we are God's handiwork, created in Christ Jesus to do good works, which God prepared in advance for us to do."* (NIV)

Philippians 1:6 *"And I am certain that God, who began the good work within you, will continue his work until it is finally finished on the day when Christ Jesus returns."*

Philippians 2:13 *"For God is working in you, giving you the desire and the power to do what pleases him."*

Acts 20:24 *"But my life is worth nothing to me unless I use it for finishing the work assigned to me by the Lord Jesus – the work of telling others the Good News about the wonderful grace of*

God."

? **A**sk: What do I find to be:

The most **A**ssuring verse(s): ________________________

How would I say the verse in my own words or language?

What does this verse mean for me? How will I live and think differently because of this verse?

My most **B**eloved verse(s): _________________________

How would I say the verse in my own words or language?

What does this verse mean for me? How will I live and think differently because of this verse?

The most **C**onvicting verse(s): ________________

How would I say the verse in my own words or language?

What does this verse mean for me? How will I live and think differently because of this verse?

⇨ Your Plan of Action: Because of what I learned today, with the Lord's help I will...

__1. Look for opportunities to do good things for other people this week.

__2. Tell ____________ the good news about God's wonderful grace today!

__3.

Remain in Prayer

Describe God
Ask forgiveness
Thank him
Express needs

Week 1, Day 4: I am **L**oved!

♥ Prepare your Heart

Lord, *"open my eyes that I may see wonderful things in your law."* (Psalm 119:18, NIV)

Read

John 15:9-13 Jesus speaking: *"I have loved you even as the Father has loved me. Remain in my love. When you obey my commandments, you remain in my love, just as I obey my Father's commandments and remain in his love. I have told you these things so that you will be filled with my joy. Yes, your joy will overflow! This is my commandment: Love each other in the same way I have loved you. There is no greater love than to lay down one's life for one's friends."*

John 17:23 Jesus speaking: *"I am in them and you are in me. May they experience such perfect unity that the world will know that you sent me and that you love them as much as you love me."*

Romans 5:8 *"But God showed his great love for us by sending Christ to die for us while we were still sinners."*

Romans 8:35-39 *"Can anything ever separate us from Christ's love? Does it mean he no longer loves us if we have trouble or calamity, or are persecuted, or hungry, or destitute, or in danger, or threatened with death? (As the Scriptures say, 'For your sake we are killed every day; we are being slaughtered like sheep.') No, despite all these things, overwhelming victory is ours through Christ, who loved us. And I am convinced that nothing can ever separate us from God's love. Neither death nor life, neither angels nor demons, neither our fears for today nor our worries about tomorrow—not even the powers of hell can separate us from God's love. No power in the sky above or in the earth below—indeed, nothing in all creation will ever be able to separate us from the love of God that is revealed in Christ Jesus our Lord."*

Ephesians 2:4-5 *"But God is so rich in mercy, and he loved us so much, that even though we were dead because of our sins, he gave us life when he raised Christ from the dead. (It is only by God's grace that you have been saved!)"*

? **A**sk: What do I find to be:

The most **A**ssuring verse(s): ______________________

How would I say the verse in my own words or language?

What does this verse mean for me? How will I live and think differently because of this verse?

My most **B**eloved verse(s): ________________________

How would I say the verse in my own words or language?

What does this verse mean for me? How will I live and think differently because of this verse?

The most **C**onvicting verse(s): _______________

How would I say the verse in my own words or language?

What does this verse mean for me? How will I live and think differently because of this verse?

⇨ Your Plan of Action: Because of what I learned today, with the Lord's help I will...

__1. Let God's love flow through me to others, by doing this today: ____________________

__2. Share what I learned today with ____________

__3.

Remain in Prayer

Describe God

Ask forgiveness

Thank him

Express needs

Week 1, Day 5: I am **I**ndwelt by Christ

[*Indwell = dwell within; live inside*]

♥ Prepare your Heart

Search my heart, Lord, and examine my motives. (See Jeremiah 17:10)

Read

John 14:20 Jesus speaking: "*When I am raised to life again, you will know that I am in my Father, and you are in me, and I am in you.*"

John 15:5 Jesus speaking: *"Yes, I am the vine; you are the branches. Those who remain in me, and I in them, will produce much fruit. For apart from me you can do nothing."*

Galatians 2:20 *"My old self has been crucified with Christ. It is no longer I who live, but Christ lives in me. So I live in this earthly body by trusting in the Son of God, who loved me and gave himself for me."*

Ephesians 3:17 *"Then Christ will make his home in your hearts as you trust in him. Your roots will grow down into God's love and keep you strong."*

Colossians 1:27 *"For God wanted them to know that the riches and glory of Christ are for you Gentiles, too. And this is the secret: Christ lives in you. This gives you assurance of sharing his glory."* ["Gentile" means any person who is not a Jew.]

? Ask: What do I find to be:

The most **A**ssuring verse(s): ______________________

How would I say the verse in my own words or language?

What does this verse mean for me? How will I live and think differently because of this verse?

My most **B**eloved verse(s): ______________________

How would I say the verse in my own words or language?

What does this verse mean for me? How will I live and think differently because of this verse?

The most **C**onvicting verse(s): _______________

How would I say the verse in my own words or language?

What does this verse mean for me? How will I live and think differently because of this verse?

⇨ Your Plan of Action: Because of what I learned today, with the Lord's help I will…

__1. Talk to Jesus throughout this day, remembering that he is not far away, but lives in me.

__2. Share what I learned today with ____________

__3.

Remain in Prayer

Describe God
Ask forgiveness
Thank him
Express needs

Week 1, Day 6: I am **F**orgiven!

♥ Prepare your Heart

May your teaching fall on me like rain, Lord; may your words refresh me like the dew of the morning! (See Deuteronomy 32:1-2)

📖 Read

Acts 10:43 *"He is the one all the prophets testified about, saying that everyone who believes in him will have their sins forgiven through his name."*

Ephesians 1:7 *"He is so rich in kindness and grace that he purchased our freedom with the blood of his Son and forgave our sins."*

Colossians 1:13-14 *"For he has rescued us from the kingdom of darkness and transferred us into the Kingdom of his dear Son, who purchased our freedom and forgave our sins."*

Colossians 2:13 *"You were dead because of your sins and because your sinful nature was not yet cut away. Then God made you alive with Christ, for he forgave all our sins."*

Colossians 3:13 *"Make allowance for each other's faults, and forgive anyone who offends you. Remember, the Lord forgave you, so you must forgive others."*

? **A**sk: What do I find to be:

The most **A**ssuring verse(s): ______________________

How would I say the verse in my own words or language?

What does this verse mean for me? How will I live and think differently because of this verse?

My most **B**eloved verse(s): ______________________

How would I say the verse in my own words or language?

What does this verse mean for me? How will I live and think differently because of this verse?

The most **C**onvicting verse(s): ______________

How would I say the verse in my own words or language?

What does this verse mean for me? How will I live and think differently because of this verse?

⇨ Your Plan of Action: Because of what I learned today, with the Lord's help I will...

__1. Forgive _______________ today, because God has forgiven every bad thing I have done, spoken, or thought.

__2. Share what I learned today with ____________

__3.

Remain in Prayer

Describe God
Ask forgiveness
Thank him
Express needs

Week 1, Day 7: I am **E**mpowered by the Holy Spirit
[*Empowered = given strength or ability*]

♥ Prepare your Heart

God, my Father, thank you for the Holy Spirit that you put in me to help me follow and obey you. (See Ezekiel 36:27)

📖 Read

Luke 24:49 Jesus speaking: *"And now I will send the Holy Spirit, just as my Father promised. But stay here in the city until the Holy Spirit comes and fills you with power from heaven."*

Acts 1:8 Jesus speaking: *"But you will receive power when the Holy Spirit comes upon you. And you will be my witnesses, telling people about me everywhere—in Jerusalem, throughout Judea, in Samaria, and to the ends of the earth."*

Galatians 5:16-26 *"So I say, let the Holy Spirit guide your lives. Then you won't be doing what your sinful nature craves. The sinful nature wants to do evil, which is just the opposite of what the Spirit wants. And the Spirit gives us desires that are the opposite of what the sinful nature desires. These two forces are constantly fighting each other, so you are not free to carry out your good intentions. But when you are directed by the Spirit, you are not under obligation to the law of Moses.*

"When you follow the desires of your sinful nature, the results are very clear: sexual immorality, impurity, lustful pleasures, idolatry, sorcery, hostility, quarreling, jealousy, outbursts of anger, selfish ambition, dissension, division, envy, drunkenness, wild parties, and other sins like these. Let me tell you again, as I

have before, that anyone living that sort of life will not inherit the Kingdom of God.

"But the Holy Spirit produces this kind of fruit in our lives: love, joy, peace, patience, kindness, goodness, faithfulness, gentleness, and self-control. There is no law against these things!

"Those who belong to Christ Jesus have nailed the passions and desires of their sinful nature to his cross and crucified them there. Since we are living by the Spirit, let us follow the Spirit's leading in every part of our lives. Let us not become conceited, or provoke one another, or be jealous of one another."

Ephesians 3:14-16 *"When I think of all this, I fall to my knees and pray to the Father, the Creator of everything in heaven and on earth. I pray that from his glorious, unlimited resources he will empower you with inner strength through his Spirit."*

Ephesians 5:18-19 *"Don't be drunk with wine, because that will ruin your life. Instead, be filled with the Holy Spirit, singing psalms and hymns and spiritual songs among yourselves, and making music to the Lord in your hearts."*

? **A**sk: What do I find to be:

The most **A**ssuring verse(s): ______________________

How would I say the verse in my own words or language?

What does this verse mean for me? How will I live and think differently because of this verse?

My most **B**eloved verse(s): ________________________

How would I say the verse in my own words or language?

What does this verse mean for me? How will I live and think differently because of this verse?

The most **C**onvicting verse(s): _______________

How would I say the verse in my own words or language?

What does this verse mean for me? How will I live and think differently because of this verse?

⇨ **Y**our Plan of Action: Because of what I learned today, with the Lord's help I will…

__1. Ask the Holy Spirit to give me the strength and courage to ______________________

__2. Share what I learned today with _____________

__3.

Remain in Prayer

Describe God

Ask forgiveness

Thank him

Express needs

Week 2: GROWING In Jesus Christ

"Wash your hands before eating." "Brush your teeth." "Wash your hands after using the bathroom." These are some of the practices our parents taught us since we were little children. Once these practices became our daily habits it got easier...and we still do these things to this day, don't we?

As a new Christian there are spiritual habits that you should develop, too. It will take practice and discipline, but if you do these things on a daily and consistent basis, you will be amazed to see yourself really *growing in Jesus Christ*!

You will be using the FLY method this week. The FLY method will help you focus on one spiritual habit each day.

FLY Method

The acronym FLY came to mind as I thought of our aviation student friends. The letters stand for "***F**ocus*", "***L**isten*", and "***Y**our response*".

Focus. Select two verses or a section of the story that you like most and copy these in your QT notebook word for word. In your Bible, look up the readings suggested here so you will become familiar with the books of the Bible. Once you have written down the verses, underline unfamiliar or difficult words or phrases. Look up their meanings. Now just focus on the verses you have chosen.

Listen. Take a few minutes to be quiet before the Lord.

He says, *"Be still, and know that I am God"* (Psalm 46:10). As you "listen" he may use the passage you just read to speak to you. He might make you aware of something in your life (actions, words, thoughts, attitudes) that he wants you to improve or eliminate. He may reveal new insights to you. He may point out a secret sin. As you wait, the Lord may bring to your mind the name of someone to pray for, or perhaps a verse you've memorized to encourage you. Psalm 85:8 says, *"I listen carefully to what God the LORD is saying, for he speaks peace to his faithful people…."*

Read those favorite verses again. Read slowly and thoughtfully. Concentrate. Then read and pray over the two verses another time. What stands out to you? Write down these things that you are hearing from the Lord.

There will be times when you might not hear from the Lord at all. This does not mean he is not listening to you. Know that he is there with you. Keep trying every day to take time to listen to him, and don't be in a hurry. *"Joyful are those who listen to me, watching for me daily…waiting for me…"* (Proverbs 8:34).

Your response. How will you respond to what you have heard from God? You might respond by thanking him for helping you to understand the verses you just focused on. Pray for that friend he brought to your mind. Thank him for the new truths you learned related to the topic of the day. Ask him to help you overcome the sin he pointed out to you. You may want to write these responses in your quiet time notebook as a prayer.

Note: ***L****isten* and ***Y****our Response* are often linked together. For example, if when you *Listen* the Lord makes you aware of a sin you committed, then *Your Response* is to confess it to him, ask his forgiveness, and try to make things right with anyone you have wronged. (To "confess" a sin means to acknowledge or admit that you are guilty of it.)

(See **Appendix A** for an example of how to do the FLY method.)

Day 1	**G**et together with Jesus every day (Quiet Time)
Day 2	**R**elate with other believers (Fellowship)
Day 3	**O**ffer back to God what he has given (Be a faithful manager)
Day 4	**W**itness for Jesus (Share the good news)
Day 5	**I**nvestigate God's word (Bible study)
Day 6	**N**ote it down (Journaling)
Day 7	**G**o and serve (Serving)

Week 2, Day 1: **G**et together with Jesus every day

I still remember a favorite children's song we used to sing in church when I was growing up in the Philippines. It went like this: *"Read your Bible, pray every day, pray every day, pray every day. Read your Bible, pray every day and you'll grow, grow, grow."* How true! I have indeed grown in my spiritual life!

Getting together with Jesus every day (Quiet Time) is not a "requirement" as much as an expression of your desire to be with someone you love and who loves you very much. As you promised to meet with him every day, know that he will be waiting for you. Make this your top priority. If possible, don't break or cancel your appointment with him. Be there!

♥ Prepare your Heart

"My heart has heard you say, 'Come and talk with me.' And my heart responds, 'LORD, I am coming.'" (Psalm 27:8)

📖 Read

Psalm 5:3 *"LORD, every morning you hear my voice. Every morning, I tell you what I need, and I wait for your answer."* (NCV)

Psalm 119:147 *"I rise early, before the sun is up; I cry out for help and put my hope in your words."*

Mark 1:32-35 *"That evening after sunset, many sick and demon-possessed people were brought to Jesus. The whole town gathered at the door to watch. So Jesus healed many people who were sick with various diseases, and he cast out many demons. But because the demons knew who he was, he did not allow them to speak. Before daybreak the next morning, Jesus got up and went out to an isolated place to pray."*

Mark 6:31-32 *"Then Jesus said, 'Let's go off by ourselves to a quiet place and rest awhile.' He said this because there were so many people coming and going that Jesus and his apostles didn't even have time to eat. So they left by boat for a quiet place, where they could be alone."*

Luke 4:42 *"Early the next morning Jesus went out to an isolated place. The crowds searched everywhere for him, and when they finally found him, they begged him not to leave them."*

Luke 6:12 *"One day soon afterward Jesus went up on a mountain to pray, and he prayed to God all night."*

? **A**sk questions that will help you understand and interact with the passage.

Focus (on two of the Bible passages above)

Listen

Your response

⇨ **Y**our Plan of Action: Because of what I learned today, with the Lord's help I will...

__1. Renew my commitment to meet with God each day.

__2. Share what I learned today with ____________

__3.

Remain in Prayer

Describe God

Ask forgiveness

Thank him

Express needs

Week 2, Day 2: **R**elate with other believers

As soon as you become a Christian, you need to find a church that believes in the Bible as the word of God and preaches from it. Connect with a Christian friend for sharing and prayer. Get involved in a Bible study or Christian fellowship group. You will be greatly helped if you can find a mature believer who can mentor you in your Christian walk. In your home country you might not know of a church, Bible study group, or even another Christian. Keep praying that the Lord will bring a brother or sister in the Lord to come along beside you. (For help in finding a church, see **Appendix C**.)

♥ Prepare your Heart

"Show me your ways, Lord, teach me your paths. Guide me in your truth and teach me, for you are God my Savior, and my hope is in you all day long." (Psalm 25:4-5, NIV)

📖 Read

Psalm 22:25 *"I will praise you in the great assembly. I will fulfill my vows in the presence of those who worship you."*

Psalm 122:1 *"I was glad when they said to me, 'Let us go to the house of the LORD.'"*

Luke 4:16 *"When he* [Jesus] *came to the village of Nazareth, his boyhood home, he went as usual to the synagogue on the Sabbath and stood up to read the Scriptures."* [A synagogue is a Jewish place of worship and spiritual instruction. "Sabbath" means Saturday, the Jewish day of rest and worship. "Scriptures" means the Bible. Jesus read from the Old Testament, which is the part of the Bible written before he came into the world.]

Acts 2:42-47 *"All the believers devoted themselves to the apostles' teaching, and to fellowship, and to sharing in meals...and to prayer. A deep sense of awe came over them all, and the apostles performed many miraculous signs and wonders. And all the believers met together in one place and shared everything they had. They sold their property and possessions and shared the money with those in need. They worshiped together at the Temple each day, met in homes for the Lord's Supper, and shared their meals with great joy and generosity—all the while praising God and enjoying the goodwill of all the people. And each day the Lord added to their fellowship those who were being saved."* ["Apostles" means here the 12 men Jesus chose to follow him, learn from him, and lead the church. He was betrayed by one of the 12—Judas Iscariot—who was later replaced by another man.]

Hebrews 10:24-25 *"Let us think of ways to motivate one another to acts of love and good works. And let us not neglect our meeting together, as some people do, but encourage one another, especially now that the day of his return is drawing near."*

? **A**sk questions that will help you interact with the passage.

Focus

Listen

Your response

➪ Your Plan of Action: Because of what I learned today, with the Lord's help I will…

__1. Try this week to find a church or Bible study group. If I already have one, I will invite any new Christians I meet who don't have such a group. (See **Appendix C**, "Finding a Church".)

__2. Share what I learned today with ____________

__3.

Remain in Prayer

Describe God
Ask forgiveness
Thank him
Express needs

Week 2, Day 3: **O**ffer back to God what he has given

"The earth is the LORD's, and everything in it, the world, and all who live in it" (Psalm 24, NIV). God owns everything… including you and me! So all that we are and all that we have belongs to him…our bodies, time, talents, skills, possessions, and money. The Bible calls us managers, not owners. We are to be good managers (or stewards) of everything God has given us. The Bible verses today will give you an understanding of your role as God's steward, or manager.

♥ Prepare your Heart

"Make me walk along the path of your commands O Lord, for that is where my happiness is found. Give me an eagerness for your laws rather than a love for money!" (Psalm 119:35-36)

📖 Read

Psalm 50:10-12 *"For all the animals of the forest are mine, and I own the cattle on a thousand hills. I know every bird on the mountains, and all the animals of the field are mine. If I were hungry, I would not tell you, for all the world is mine and everything in it."*

1 Corinthians 4:2 *"Now, a person who is put in charge as a manager must be faithful."*

1 Corinthians 16:2 *"On the first day of every week, each one of you should set aside a sum of money in keeping with your income, saving it up, so that when I come no collections will have to be made."* (NIV)

Romans 12:1 *"Therefore, I urge you, brothers and sisters, in view of God's mercy, to offer your bodies as a living sacrifice, holy and pleasing to God—this is your true and proper worship."* (NIV)

Romans 14:12 *"Yes, each of us will give a personal account to God."*

1 Peter 4:10 *"God has given each of you a gift from his great variety of spiritual gifts. Use them well to serve one another."*

? Ask questions that will help you interact with the passage.

Focus

Listen

Your response

➪ Your Plan of Action: Because of what I learned today, with the Lord's help I will…

__1. Set aside _______________ from my wages this month and give it to God.

__2. Share what I learned today with ____________

__3.

Remain in Prayer

Describe God
Ask forgiveness
Thank him
Express needs

Week 2, Day 4: **W**itness for Jesus

[*To witness something means to see or experience it ourselves. Christians also use the word to mean telling others the good news about Jesus, whom we know personally.*]

When you find a good restaurant or watch a great movie, do you tell other people about it? Of course! You want them to enjoy it just as you did. The final instructions Jesus gave before he left this earth were that we should share the good news of salvation to everyone! Your family, friends, and workmates need to hear about Jesus. You may be the only representative of him that they meet. Don't be pushy about it, but look for opportunities to tell them about Jesus Christ and his offer of eternal life.

♥ Prepare your Heart

Lord, help me live life in a way that you would consider worthy. (See I Thessalonians 2:12)

🕮 Read

Acts 1:8 *"But you will receive power when the Holy Spirit comes upon you. And you will be my witnesses, telling people about me everywhere—in Jerusalem, throughout Judea, in Samaria, and to the ends of the earth."*

Matthew 28:19-20 *"Therefore, go and make disciples of all the nations, baptizing them in the name of the Father and the Son and the Holy Spirit. Teach these new disciples to obey all the commands I have given you. And be sure of this: I am with you always, even to the end of the age."*

2 Corinthians 2:15 *"For we are to God the pleasing aroma of Christ among those who are being saved and those who are perishing."* (NIV)

Colossians 4:5-6 *"Be wise in the way you act toward outsiders; make the most of every opportunity. Let your conversation be always full of grace, seasoned with salt, so that you may know how to answer everyone."* (NIV)

2 Timothy 4:5 *"But you should keep a clear mind in every situation. Don't be afraid of suffering for the Lord. Work at telling others the Good News, and fully carry out the ministry God has given you."*

1 Peter 3:15 *"Instead, you must worship Christ as Lord of your life. And if someone asks about your Christian hope, always be ready to explain it. But do this in a gentle and respectful way. Keep your conscience clear. Then if people speak against you, they will be ashamed when they see what a good life you live because you belong to Christ."*

? Ask questions that will help you interact with the passage.

Focus

Listen

Your response

⇨ **Y**our Plan of Action: Because of what I learned today, with the Lord's help I will...

__1. Memorize 2 Timothy 4:5 today.

__2. Talk to ____________ this week about what Jesus has

done for me.

__3.

Remain in Prayer

Describe God

Ask forgiveness

Thank him

Express needs

Week 2, Day 5: **I**nvestigate God's word

[*Investigate = examine, observe, inquire, study*]

My husband has been researching his family history. He looks at old documents and pictures, visits gravesites, talks with older relatives, and takes time to get accurate information. His thorough study has uncovered new and interesting facts that even his parents were not aware of. It brings him great excitement when he learns new information about his ancestors.

The goal of Bible study is to uncover spiritual truths from God's word through carefully observing the text, properly interpreting it, and applying to life what is learned. Since the goal of this book is to help you be established in your Quiet Time, today you will find what the Bible says about studying God's word.

♥ Prepare your Heart

"I will study your commandments and reflect on your ways. I will delight in your decrees and not forget your word." (Psalm 119:15-16)

📖 Read

Psalm 119:11 *"I have hidden your word in my heart that I might not sin against you."* (NIV)

Proverbs 22:17-18 *"Listen to the words of the wise; apply your heart to my instruction. For it is good to keep these sayings in your heart and always ready on your lips."*

Acts 17:11 *"Now the Berean Jews were of more noble character than those in Thessalonica, for they received the message with great eagerness and examined the Scriptures every day to see if what Paul said was true."* (NIV)

2 Timothy 2:15 *"Work hard so you can present yourself to God and receive his approval. Be a good worker, one who does not need to be ashamed and who correctly explains the word of truth."*

2 Timothy 3:16 *"All Scripture is inspired by God and is useful to teach us what is true and to make us realize what is wrong in our lives. It corrects us when we are wrong and teaches us to do what is right."* [inspired = breathed]

1 Peter 2:2 *"Like babies that were just born, you should long for the pure milk of God's word. It will help you grow up as believers."* (NIrV®)

Romans 15:4 *"Such things were written in the Scriptures long ago to teach us. And the Scriptures give us hope and encouragement as we wait patiently for God's promises to be fulfilled."*

? Ask questions that will help you interact with the passage.

Focus

Listen

Your response

⇨ Your Plan of Action: Because of what I learned today, with the Lord's help I will...

__1. Memorize Psalm 119:11 today.

__2. Commit myself to studying the Bible on my own every day, and with others every week.

__3.

Remain in Prayer

Describe God
Ask forgiveness
Thank him
Express needs

Week 2, Day 6: **N**ote it down

I have practiced the habit of journaling for over 30 years. I've kept a record of lessons I learned from the Lord, as well as my prayers, doubts, questions, joys, heartaches, expressions of thanks, and more. So many times I have gone back to read what I wrote five or even 20 years ago. I've always been encouraged. There are times when I lift thoughts from my notebook to share with someone who needs the very encouragement I needed at that particular day some time back. It also helps me see my growth in the knowledge of God's word as well as in my love for him. I hope you'll give journaling a try.

♥ Prepare your Heart

Lord, I seek you while I can find you. I will call on you now while you are near. (See Isaiah 55:6)

📖 Read

Exodus 24:4 *"Then Moses carefully wrote down all the LORD's instructions."*

Psalm 102:18 *"Write these things for the future so that people who are not yet born will praise the Lord."* (NCV)

Jeremiah 30:2 *"This is what the LORD, the God of Israel, says: Write down for the record everything I have said to you, Jeremiah."*

Luke 1:3 *"Having carefully investigated everything from the beginning, I also have decided to write a careful account for you...."*

John 21:24 *"This disciple is the one who testifies to these events and has recorded them here. And we know that his account of these things is accurate."*

? **A**sk questions that will help you interact with the passage.

Focus

Listen

Your response

⇨ **Y**our Plan of Action: Because of what I learned today, with the Lord's help I will…

__1. Begin journaling today.

__2.

Remain in Prayer

Describe God

Ask forgiveness

Thank him

Express needs

Week 2, Day 7: **G**o and serve

When Jesus was on earth he lived a life of service. He healed, he taught, and he comforted those who were sad. When you decided to put your faith in Jesus, the Holy Spirit gave you one or more spiritual gifts for the purpose of serving other believers. What do you think your spiritual gift (or gifts) may be? Ask God to show you, and be faithful in using your gifts for him.

♥ Prepare your Heart

Lord, fill my heart with your light so I will understand the hope you have given me. (See Ephesians 1:18)

📖 Read

Romans 12:7-8 *"If your gift is serving others, serve them well. If you are a teacher, teach well. If your gift is to encourage others, be encouraging. If it is giving, give generously. If God has given you leadership ability, take the responsibility seriously. And if you have a gift for showing kindness to others, do it gladly."*

Romans 12:11-13 *"Never be lazy, but work hard and serve the Lord enthusiastically. Rejoice in our confident hope. Be patient in trouble, and keep on praying. When God's people are in need, be ready to help them. Always be eager to practice hospitality."*

1 Peter 4:8-11 *"Most important of all, continue to show deep love for each other, for love covers a multitude of sins. Cheerfully share your home with those who need a meal or a place to stay. God has given each of you a gift from his great variety of spiritual gifts. Use them well to serve one another. Do you have the gift of speaking? Then speak as though God himself were speaking through you. Do you have the gift of helping others? Do it with all the strength and energy that God supplies. Then everything you do will bring glory to God through Jesus Christ. All glory and power to him forever and ever! Amen."*

? **A**sk questions that will help you interact with the passage.

Focus

Listen

Your response

⇨ **Y**our Plan of Action: Because of what I learned today, with the Lord's help I will…

__1. This week I will ask other Christians who know me, "What spiritual gift do you see in me?"

__2. Today I will serve someone in this way: ________________________________

__3.

Remain in Prayer

Describe God
Ask forgiveness
Thank him
Express needs

Week 3: WALKING with Jesus

Once your family, friends or co-workers know you have become a Christian, they will be watching you. An American saying goes, "Walk the talk." That is, your actions should agree with what you say. For example, people will observe how you respond to things such as temptation to sin, losing a job, mistreatment from your boss, and so on. Do they see anger in you? Worry? Fear? Disobedience toward God? Or do they see your inner joy, strength, peace, trust, forgiveness, and goodness? How you handle life's difficulties will speak loudly about your faith, and it will influence their opinions about Jesus.

Your QT portions are stories taken from the four Gospels (Matthew, Mark, Luke and John) about men and women who faced some of the same problems you and I face. You will be encouraged as you see how Jesus helped them. This week, try reading the story out loud so you can hear yourself.

PURE Method

You can use this method when you are reading stories in the Bible. PURE method asks you to:

Pick out a character in the story with whom you want to identify. You may want to be the main character, one of the disciples, a member of the crowd, etc. Now imagine that you are that character while you read the story again.

Uncover the feelings and emotions of your character. Feel what he or she is feeling. Are you afraid? Happy?

Amazed? Hurting? Sad? Do you feel ashamed? Unloved? Excited? Desperate? Thankful? What are you thinking as you watch a miracle unfold before your eyes? How did that affect you? Who and what do you see, hear, and smell? Is it crowded? What do you observe about people's actions and responses? Do you hear the authority in Jesus' voice? Write or think about the story from your character's perspective.

Reflect on the story. In what ways are you like or not like the character you've chosen? How would you have responded if you were there? What did Jesus say and do that made an impression on you? What impressed you about the character you've chosen?

Express in prayer what you just learned. Write your prayer down.

(See **Appendix A** for an example of how to do the PURE method.)

Day 1 In my **W**orries... he cares deeply
Day 2 In my **A**ffliction... he identifies completely
Day 3 In my **L**ongings... he satisfies fully
Day 4 My un**K**nown future... he offers security
Day 5 In my **I**nsignificance... he values me highly
Day 6 In my **N**eeds... he provides faithfully
Day 7 In my **G**rief... he offers hope

Week 3, Day 1: In my **W**orries and fears...he cares deeply

♥ Prepare your Heart

"Teach me your decrees, O Lord; I will keep them to the end. Give me understanding and I will obey your instructions; I will

put them into practice with all my heart." (Psalm 119:33-34)

📖 Read

Mark 4:35-41 (The worried disciples)

? Ask questions that will help you interact with the passage.

Pick out a character.

Uncover the feelings of your character.

Reflect on the story.

Express in prayer what Jesus taught you from this passage. Write your prayer down.

⇨ Your Plan of Action: Because of what I learned today, with the Lord's help I will…

__1. Memorize Mark 4:39 today.

__2. Stop worrying about ________________ and trust God with the situation.

__3.

Remain in Prayer

Describe God

Ask forgiveness

Thank him

Express needs

Week 3, Day 2: In my **A**ffliction…he identifies completely

[*Affliction = suffering, pain, trouble, or distress*]

♥ Prepare your Heart

"I delight in your instructions. My suffering was good for me, for it taught me to pay attention to your decrees. Your instructions are more valuable to me than millions in gold and silver." (Psalm 119:70-72)

Read

Mark 5:21-34 (The afflicted woman)

? Ask questions that will help you interact with the passage.

Pick out a character.

Uncover the feelings of your character.

Reflect on the story.

Express in prayer what Jesus taught you from this passage. Write your prayer down.

➪ Your Plan of Action: Because of what I learned today, with the Lord's help I will…

__1. Ask Jesus to help me with this problem: ________________________, knowing that he is greater than my problems.

__2. Tell ____________ today about a prayer that God has answered for me.

__3.

Remain in Prayer

Describe God
Ask forgiveness
Thank him
Express needs

Week 3, Day 3: In my **L**ongings…he satisfies fully

[*Longings = deep desires or strong wishes*]

♥ Prepare your Heart

"I am exhausted and completely crushed. My groans come from an anguished heart. You know what I long for, Lord; you hear my every sigh." (Psalm 38:8-9)

📖 **R**ead John 5:1-15 (A crippled man healed)

? Ask questions that will help you interact with the passage.

Pick out a character.

Uncover the feelings of your character.

Reflect on the story.

Express in prayer what Jesus taught you from this passage. Write your prayer down.

➪ **Y**our Plan of Action: Because of what I learned today, with the Lord's help I will…

__1. Ask God to heal ____________________

__2. Give praise to Jesus who can not only heal bodies, but (more importantly) forgive sins!

__3.

Remain in Prayer

Describe God

Ask forgiveness

Thank him

Express needs

Week 3, Day 4: In my un**K**nown future…he offers security

♥ Prepare your Heart

"My future is in your hands. Rescue me from those who hunt me down relentlessly." (Psalm 31:15)

Read Luke 5:1-11 (A disciple's future told)

? Ask questions that will help you interact with the passage.

Pick out a character.

Uncover the feelings of your character.

Reflect on the story.

Express in prayer what Jesus taught you from this passage. Write your prayer down.

➪ Your Plan of Action: Because of what I learned today, with the Lord's help I will…

__1. Memorize Luke 5:11 today.

__2. Ask God to prepare me for whatever future he has planned for me.

__3.

Remain in Prayer

Describe God
Ask forgiveness
Thank him
Express needs

Week 3, Day 5: In my **I**nsignificance…he values me highly

♥ Prepare your Heart

You said, *"I have called you by name; you are mine…you are precious to me. You are honored, and I love you"* (Isaiah 43:1 & 4). How reassuring your words are to me, O Lord!

Read Luke 18:35-43 (A blind beggar receives his sight)

? Ask questions that will help you interact with the passage.

Pick out a character.

Uncover the feelings of your character.

Reflect on the story.

Express in prayer what Jesus taught you from this passage. Write your prayer down.

⇨ Your Plan of Action: Because of what I learned today, with the Lord's help I will...

__1. Refuse to think too poorly of myself today, knowing that in spite of my failures and weaknesses God loves me and values me as his precious child.

__2. Be very clear and specific in my prayers this week.

__3.

Remain in Prayer

Describe God
Ask forgiveness
Thank him
Express needs

Week 3, Day 6: In my **N**eeds…he provides faithfully

♥ Prepare your Heart

Lord, you are my shepherd; you give me everything I need (see Psalm 23:1). Teach me to trust you more!

🕮 Read Luke 9:10-17 (Feeding of the 5,000)

? Ask questions that will help you interact with the passage.

Pick out a character.

Uncover the feelings of your character.

Reflect on the story.

Express in prayer what Jesus taught you from this passage. Write your prayer down.

⇨ Your Plan of Action: Because of what I learned today, with the Lord's help I will…

__1. Confidently ask him to supply all my needs.

__2. Encourage a fellow Christian to trust God this week, reminding him or her about this miracle that Jesus did.

__3.

Remain in Prayer

Describe God
Ask forgiveness
Thank him
Express needs

Week 3, Day 7: In my **G**rief...he offers hope

My mother died in a bus accident when I was 17 years old. My first husband died unexpectedly when he was in his thirties. I have known deep grief...but I have also known hope! God comforted me in my sorrow with his presence; with the assurance that he would take care of me; and with his wonderful promise that those who belong to him will live with him forever.

♥ Prepare your Heart

I love you, Lord; you are my strength. You are my rock, my fortress, and my Savior...you are my shield...and my place of safety. (See Psalm 18:1-2)

Read John 11:17-44 (The Grieving Sisters)

? Ask questions that will help you interact with the passage.

Pick out a character.

Uncover the feelings of your character.

Reflect on the story.

Express in prayer what Jesus taught you from this passage. Write your prayer down.

⇨ Your Plan of Action: Because of what I learned today, with the Lord's help I will…

__1. Give thanks to God that I don't have to fear what will happen to me after my body dies, because he has promised me life with him that will never end.

__2. Memorize John 11:25-26 today.

__3.

Remain in Prayer

Describe God
Ask forgiveness
Thank him
Express needs

Week 4: The JOURNEY Ahead

The Christian life is a journey. The road ahead is sometimes smooth, sometimes rocky; sometimes flat, sometimes steep. At times you might face rejection, persecution, and trouble. But Jesus said, *"Do not let your hearts be troubled….If the world hates you, keep in mind that it hated me first"* (John 14:1 & 15:18, NIV).

While you're on this journey, always trust the Lord Jesus, because he is the best guide you can ever have. Don't give up when things are not going your way. Don't turn away from him to follow false gods, or to follow your own desires. Stay with him! He is in control, and he knows what lies ahead.

Your Quiet Times this week will teach and encourage you to go through the journey of life successfully.

PICTURES method

This week you will try a method called PICTURES. Read the passage slowly and prayerfully, then read it again. As in the other methods, look up the meaning of words that are unfamiliar to you. Think deeply about the text by asking the following PICTURES questions. Is there a…

Promise I can hold on to?

Instruction I should obey?

Challenge I need to face?

Truth about God that's new to me?

Unanswered question I should find out?

Rebuke I should pay attention to? [*rebuke = sharp word of correction*]

Encouraging word?

Sin I should confess?

For instance, as you're reading the Bible verses, one verse may be just the promise you need from the Lord that day. Write the verse under "**P**romise." Take time to think about the verse or verses you've chosen before moving on. Another verse might point out a sin which you know you need to confess to God. At that moment, admit your sin to the Lord and ask for his forgiveness. When you see an encouraging verse, thank him. Write the verse under "**E**ncouraging word." If the Lord challenges you to restore a broken relationship, write the verses under "**C**hallenge I need to face" and ask the Lord to give you the determination to do it! If he instructs you to "rid yourselves of filthy language from your lips" ask the Lord to give you the strength to obey. Write the verse under "**I**nstruction I should obey"... and so on.

(See **Appendix A** for an example of how to do the PICTURES method.)

Day 1	**J**oy in trials and suffering
Day 2	**O**bedience and faith
Day 3	**U**ndivided loyalty
Day 4	**R**esist temptation
Day 5	**N**ever give up
Day 6	**E**xample (be a good one!)
Day 7	**Y**ielded life

Week 4, Day 1: Joy in trials and suffering

How can you be joyful in the midst of trials and suffering? How can you be joyful when you fail your final exams and this may end your career dreams? Or when your father loses his job, or your sister is diagnosed with cancer? What if you are put into prison because of your faith? After Jesus left the earth, many of his followers faced severe persecution. This still happens in many countries. Yet we find believers rejoicing and praising God in the midst of trouble and suffering. One such example is that of Paul and Silas in Acts 16.

♥ **P**repare your Heart

Hear me Lord, and have mercy on me. Turn my sadness into joyful dancing. Take away my clothes of mourning and dress me up in joy, that I may sing praises to you. My God, I will give you praise forever! (See Psalm 30:10-12)

📖 **R**ead Acts 16:16-34 (Paul and Silas)

? **A**sk questions that will help you interact with the passage. Is there a…

Promise I can hold on to?

Instruction I should obey?

Challenge I need to face?

Truth about God that's new to me?

Unanswered question I should find out?

Rebuke I should pay attention to?

Encouraging word?

Sin I should confess?

⇨ **Y**our Plan of Action: Because of what I learned today, with the Lord's help I will...

__1. Rejoice and be thankful this week, even though I'm facing this problem: ________________

__2. Not hide the fact that I am a follower of Jesus, even if it might cause me trouble.

__3.

Remain in Prayer

Describe God

Ask forgiveness

Thank him

Express needs

(To learn more about having joy in trials and suffering, you can look at Matthew 5:11-12; John 15:19-23; 1 Thessalonians 5:16-18; James 1:2-4; 1 Peter 1:6, 7; and 1 Peter 4:12-16.)

Week 4, Day 2: **O**bedience

Christians are called to a life of obedience. Jesus said, *"If you love me, obey my commandments"* (John 14:15). Obeying him is not easy, but it is necessary. It is also *possible*, because God's Spirit gives us the strength to obey him.

An extreme example of obedience is the story of Abraham. He was asked by God to give up that which was most precious to him, and he obeyed without question. Would you do the same? Today's Bible passage will encourage you to live in total obedience to the Lord Jesus.

♥ Prepare your Heart

Lord, help me to not only listen to your word, but also to do what it says. (See James 1:22)

Read Genesis 22:1-19 (Abraham and Isaac)

? Ask questions that will help you interact with the passage. Is there a...

Promise I can hold on to?

Instruction I should obey?

Challenge I need to face?

Truth about God that's new to me?

Unanswered question I should find out?

Rebuke I should pay attention to?

Encouraging word?

Sin I should confess?

⇨ **Y**our Plan of Action: Because of what I learned today, with the Lord's help I will…

__1. Obey God's word today in this way:
______________________________, knowing that he will reward me for obeying.

__2. Thank God the Father today for loving us enough to sacrifice his only Son, Jesus, so that we could have eternal life.

__3.

Remain in Prayer

Describe God
Ask forgiveness
Thank him
Express needs

(To learn more about obedience, you can look at Joshua 1:8; Matt 7:21 & 24; John 14:15, 21, & 24; Acts 5:29; and 1 John 2:3-6.)

Week 4, Day 3: **U**ndivided allegiance

When I became a U.S. citizen, I pledged my oath of allegiance to my new country and renounced all of my allegiance to the country in which I was born. I felt emotional at the proceedings because of my attachment to my native land, yet I had already made the decision and I was not going to turn back.

In the same way, when you turn your life over to Jesus, he should receive your undivided loyalty. Your QT portion today highlights three young men who made up their minds to be loyal and faithful to the one true God—even if it meant death.

♥ Prepare your Heart

"Bend down, O LORD, and hear my prayer; answer me, for I need your help. Protect me, for I am devoted to you. Save me, for I serve you and trust you. You are my God." (Psalm 86:1-2)

📖 Read Daniel 3 (Story of three friends)

? Ask questions that will help you interact with the passage. Is there a...

Promise I can hold on to?

Instruction I should obey?

Challenge I need to face?

Truth about God that's new to me?

Unanswered question I should find out?

Rebuke I should pay attention to?

Encouraging word?

Sin I should confess?

Your Plan of Action: Because of what I learned today, with the Lord's help I will…

__1. Ask God to show me this week if there are any ways I am not being loyal to him.

__2. Read Daniel 3:17-18 at least three different times throughout the day today.

__3.

Remain in Prayer

Describe God
Ask forgiveness
Thank him
Express needs

(To learn more about giving God your undivided allegiance, you can look at Matthew 6:24; Matthew 10:37-39; and James 4:4.)

Week 4, Day 4: **R**esist temptation

The Bible warns us to *"Stay alert! Watch out for your great enemy, the devil. He prowls around like a roaring lion looking for someone to devour. Stand firm against him, and be strong in your faith"* (I Peter 5:9, 10). We all face temptation. In your new life as a follower of Jesus, be aware of Satan's tricks and schemes. He knows your weaknesses. He will try to entice you back to the old life you once lived. But do not give in! Resist him. Are you tempted by wealth? Pornography? Overeating? Jealousy? Power? Pride? Sex outside of marriage?

Joseph was tempted day after day by his master's wife. As the wife of a rich and powerful man, she was probably beautiful. It would have been easier for Joseph to give in than to resist her. What would you do in a similar situation? What can you learn from Joseph?

♥ **P**repare your Heart

Lord, *"Come and show me your mercy, as you do for all who love your name. Guide my steps by your word, so I will not be overcome by evil."* (Psalm 119:132-133)

🕮 **R**ead Genesis 39 (Joseph)

? **A**sk questions that will help you interact with the passage. Is there a...

Promise I can hold on to?

Instruction I should obey?

Challenge I need to face?

Truth about God that's new to me?

Unanswered question I should find out?

Rebuke I should pay attention to?

Encouraging word?

Sin I should confess?

⇨ **Y**our Plan of Action: Because of what I learned today, with the Lord's help I will…

__1. Say "no" to this temptation which I have not been resisting: ________________

__2. Avoid this place or situation which causes me temptation: ________________

__3.

Remain in Prayer

Describe God

Ask forgiveness
Thank him
Express needs

(To learn more about resisting temptation, you can look at 1 Corinthians 10:13; 2 Timothy 2:22; James 1:13-14; 1 Peter 2:12; and 1 Peter 5:8.)

Week 4, Day 5: **N**ever give up!

It's easy to give up when things don't go our way. In your Christian journey you will face many difficulties, obstacles, and seemingly unanswered prayers. You might lose friends and loved ones who reject you because of your faith. You might be the only believer in your town and you may have been searching for a church or even one other Christian with whom you can have fellowship, but your search has been fruitless so far. Perhaps you have been praying for your family members to know the Lord, but their hearts are not yet open to him. You might become discouraged and feel like giving up, but remember what Paul said: *"So let's not get tired of doing what is good. At just the right time we will reap a harvest of blessing if we don't give up"* (Galatians 6:9).

♥ Prepare your Heart
Lord, *"You are good and do only good; please teach me your decrees"* today. (Psalm 119:68).

📖 Read Job 1:1 – 2:13; 42:10-17 (Job)

? Ask questions that will help you interact with the passage.

Is there a...

Promise I can hold on to?

Instruction I should obey?

Challenge I need to face?

Truth about God that's new to me?

Unanswered question I should find out?

Rebuke I should pay attention to?

Encouraging word?

Sin I should confess?

⇨ Your Plan of Action: Because of what I learned today, with the Lord's help I will…

__1. Trust in God's goodness in spite of ____________________

__2. Memorize Job 1:21

__3.

Remain in Prayer

Describe God
Ask forgiveness
Thank him
Express needs

(To learn more about not giving up, you can look at Luke 18:1; 1 Corinthians 15:58; 2 Corinthians 4:1-18; Galatians 6:9; and Hebrews 12: 1-3.)

Week 4, Day 6: Be an **E**xample

Now that you are a member of God's family, there are those still younger in faith who will be looking up to you as a role model for how to live as a Christian. We all have a responsibility to set a good example for others. In I Timothy 4:12, Paul urges his disciple, Timothy: *"Don't let anyone think less of you because you are young. Be an example to all believers in what you say, in the way you live, in your love, your faith, and your purity."*

♥ Prepare your Heart

God my Father, thank you that you love me and have chosen me to be your own. Help me to become a good example to all the believers where I live and work. (See 1 Thessalonians 1:4-7)

📖 **R**ead Titus 2:1-15 (Paul's instructions to Titus)

? **A**sk questions that will help you interact with the passage.
Is there a…

Promise I can hold on to?

Instruction I should obey?

Challenge I need to face?

Truth about God that's new to me?

Unanswered question I should find out?

Rebuke I should pay attention to?

Encouraging word?

Sin I should confess?

⇨ **Y**our Plan of Action: Because of what I learned today, with the Lord's help I will…

__1. Try to set a better example for others in this way:

____

__2.

__3.

Remain in Prayer

Describe God

Ask forgiveness

Thank him

Express needs

(To learn more about being a good example, you can look at Philippians 3:17 and Colossians 4:5-6.)

Week 4, Day 7: **Y**ielded life

To "yield" to God is to give up your rights, to submit, to surrender, to give in to his will. He is Lord of all, so we must obey him. Yielding our lives to him may cost us our job, our reputation, our possessions, our freedom…or even our lives. Jesus yielded to the will of his Heavenly Father. Just before he was arrested, he prayed, "*My Father! If it is possible, let this cup of suffering be taken away from me. Yet I want your will to be done, not mine"* (Matthew 26:39).

Daniel also lived a surrendered life. His story is very encouraging, as you will see.

♥ Prepare your Heart

"I will keep on obeying your instructions forever and ever. I will walk in freedom, for I have devoted myself to your commandments." (Psalm 119:44-45)

📖 Read Daniel 6 (Daniel in the lions' den)

? Ask questions that will help you interact with the passage. Is there a...

Promise I can hold on to?

Instruction I should obey?

Challenge I need to face?

Truth about God that's new to me?

Unanswered question I should find out?

Rebuke I should pay attention to?

Encouraging word?

Sin I should confess?

Your Plan of Action: Because of what I learned today, with the Lord's help I will...

__1. Surrender my future plans to God and be willing to follow him however he leads me.

__2. Tell the story of Daniel to ____________

__3.

Remain in Prayer

Describe God
Ask forgiveness
Thank him
Express needs

(To learn more about living a yielded life, you can look at Romans 12:1-2; Galatians 2:20; Galatians 5:24; and Colossians 2:6-7.)

Week 5: On Your Own

Day 1	Mark 1: 1-8
Day 2	Mark 1: 9-15
Day 3	Mark 1: 16 to…? (You decide!)
Day 4	Mark
Day 5	Mark
Day 6	Mark
Day 7	Mark

This week you can choose from the four methods you've learned (ABC, FLY, PURE, or PICTURES). You may use one Quiet Time method for each day, or use your favorite method for the whole week. It's all up to you!

For your practice Quiet Times, we have been jumping from one book of the Bible to another. From now on, though, you will normally want to continue in one book (such as Mark) until you have finished it. This is important for understanding the full message of the book and for correctly interpreting each verse and passage within its context.

A word of advice: A friend may give you a daily Bible reading guide (such as "Daily Bread" or "The Upper Room") to use for your Quiet Time. In it you'll see a Bible passage and comments of the writers. If you plan to use that, I suggest that you proceed with PRAY'R first, reading the suggested passage for the day, selecting from the 4 methods already familiar to you and only after that should you read the author's comments. You want to hear from the Lord first before being influenced by another person's thoughts.

So go ahead, get your notebook ready, and open your Bible to the Gospel of Mark. Depending on your Bible translation, you may find that each chapter is divided into paragraphs and sections, or it might be organized under subtitles. You might want to read a whole chapter at once, or you might just read one or two sections within a chapter. Again…it's up to you. I've given you the Scripture sections for Days 1, 2 and 3. After that, you are on your own…but not really, because the Holy Spirit is in you!

Part 3 - My Prayer Organizer

Section A is a short discussion on **DATE praying**.

Section B is your **prayer list**.

Section C is a place to record your **prayer requests and answers**.

Section A: DATE Praying

I hear questions and comments like: "I don't know how to pray", "How should I pray?", and "What should I pray?" Put simply, prayer is having a conversation with the Lord. You talk to him. You listen to him. He speaks to you through his word. You obey what he says! It's like a pilot communicating with the Air Traffic Controller about his situation. Both of them understand each other and the pilot follows the Controller's instructions.

DATE praying is a pattern you can follow when you pray during your Quiet Time, or when praying with other people. Start your prayer time by praising God. How?

Describe God. If you are describing the leader of your country, what words come to your mind? Hopefully you can say he is honest. He loves his people. He is just. He is humble. Now, how about describing God? What can you say about him? Here are a few of the things the Bible says about God's character and qualities: He is the creator. He is forgiving. He is just. He is love. He loved us so much he sent Jesus, his only Son. He knows all things and has all wisdom. He is holy. He is strong and mighty. He is patient, compassionate, and kind.

In other words, this is a time to worship and praise God. Take delight in Him! For example, you might honor God by expressing how much you appreciate him, like this:

"Father, you are faithful. You are always true to your promises. You never fail. I love you so much!"

"Lord Jesus, I worship you because you are holy and pure! You are full of grace and truth!"

"I praise you, God, because you protect your children. You are my fortress and my deliverer. You preserved my life from a deadly crash this morning! You are so awesome!"

(I keep an alphabetical list of God's qualities and characteristics that I find in the Bible. Every time I notice a verse or word that refers to who God is, I add this to the list. I often use this list in my worship time. You may want to start one!)

Here are a few examples of how to praise and worship the Lord: Psalm 103, Psalm 104, Psalm 145, Daniel 4:32.

When I worship God and think about his goodness, it reminds me that I need to be washed clean from any sins which I have not yet confessed to him. This leads me to...

Ask forgiveness. Jesus taught his disciples to pray, *"Forgive us for our sins, just as we have forgiven those who sinned against us"* (Matthew 6:12, NCV). The Bible says that because of sin, God will not hear our prayers (see Isaiah 59:1-2). So like King

David who said, *"I confessed all my sins to you and stopped trying to hide my guilt"* (Psalm 32:5), open your heart to him. Specifically mention any sin that you have not addressed during your Quiet Time. Admit to that sin and ask for his forgiveness. Pray 1 John 1:9, *"Lord I confess my sin of ___________. Thank you that you are faithful and just and will forgive my sin and purify me from all unrighteousness. I believe that you have forgiven me because you are true to your word."*

Thank God. Now thank him for small and big blessings—the beauty of his creation, the air you breathe, the food you eat, your job, and so on. Thank him for your parents, friends, or children. Thank him even when things go badly for you, for the Bible says *"give thanks in all circumstances; for this is God's will for you in Christ Jesus"* (I Thessalonians 5:18, NIV). Thank him for what he has done for you...setting you free from being a captive to sin, and giving you eternal life. Thank him for what he is doing in your life now...like giving you opportunities to share his love with others, positive changes you are seeing in your attitudes and behavior, and so on. What else can you thank the Lord for?

Express needs. Jesus also taught his disciples to express their needs to God by praying things like, "give us today our daily bread..." (Matthew 6:11, NIV). This is now the time to pray for the needs of yourself, your family, friends, and others. Go to your Prayer List (see **Section B: My Prayer List** below) and pray for those in your list that day.

When you pray for your needs, tell the Lord everything! Share your deepest longings, fears, heartaches, plans, etc. *"This is the confidence we have in approaching God: that if we ask anything according to his will, he hears us"* (1 John 5:14, NIV). It's good to include Scriptures in your prayers. For instance, if you are making decisions, ask him to guide and direct you. You can quote Proverbs 3:5-6 and make it personal, like: *"Lord, I trust you with all my heart. I only want to rely on you, and not on my own understanding. Please make my path straight. I need your wisdom as I make this important decision."* I also like to write my prayers. Try it!

Section B: My Prayer List

As I grew in my Christian walk, my list of people to pray for also grew! I found it helpful to organize my prayer time using a list. I pray for the people I care about most on certain days of the week. So find a time when you can create this list (not during your QT period!). You may find the following suggestions helpful:

1. Take some paper and list the names of people for whom you are praying, or for whom you want to start praying.

2. Group them into seven categories—one for each day of the week. (See the example below for some ideas about how you might do that.)

3. Decide which day of the week you want to pray for these groups.

<u>SUNDAY: My Church Family</u>

Pastor/Leader
Pastor's wife & family
Elders & Deacons (church leaders)
Teachers
All members

<u>MONDAY: My Family</u>

Parents

Brothers/Sisters

Husband/Wife

Children

Relatives

<u>TUESDAY: Local Friends</u>

Work Friends
School Friends
Bible Study group
Neighbors

Other friends

<u>WEDNESDAY: My Job</u>

Boss

Co-workers

Company

Clients/Customers

THURSDAY: Government Officials

"First, I tell you to pray for all people, asking God for what they need and being thankful to him. Pray for rulers and for all who have authority so that we can have quiet and peaceful lives full of worship and respect for God. This is good, and it pleases God our Savior, who wants all people to be saved and to know the truth" (1 Timothy 2:1-4, NCV).

My President/Prime Minister
City Officials
Judges
Other Officials

<u>FRIDAY: My Friends Abroad</u>

<u>SATURDAY: Others</u>

Section C: Prayer Requests & Answers

"Don't worry about anything, but pray about everything. With thankful hearts offer up your prayers and requests to God" (Philippians 4:6, CEV).

God hears your prayers! Sometimes he answers immediately. Other times he will not answer as quickly as you want him to, and he might not always answer in the way that you want. But he is your loving, caring, all-wise, all-knowing Father. He knows the future, and he knows what is truly best for you.

My prayer life has grown deep and strong from seeing the wonderful things God has done. He has answered so many prayers that I could never remember them all. But I remember many of them, because I keep a list of his answers. When I read them, my faith grows and I want to pray even more!

I suggest that you use a notebook to keep a list like the one below. Write your prayer requests and the dates you started praying on the left side of the page. On the right side you will write God's answer to that request and the date it was answered. By doing this simple thing, you will see at a glance the many times God has answered your prayers. In the future, as you review those pages to see how God answered your prayers, you will be very encouraged! For it is true that *"the earnest prayer of a righteous person has great power and produces wonderful results"* (James 5:16).

Example:

DATE	REQUEST	ANSWER (when & how)
6/30/15	Lee needs a job.	7/22/15 Hired by software company!

Appendix A

Examples of Four Quiet Time Methods

(The examples will only give you the Read and Ask sections of the PRAY'R format.)

Example of ABC Method

📖 Read Psalm 1

1 *Happy are those who don't listen to the wicked,*
who don't go where sinners go,
who don't do what evil people do.
2 *They love the LORD's teachings,*
and they think about those teachings day and night.
3 *They are strong, like a tree planted by a river.*
The tree produces fruit in season,
and its leaves don't die.
Everything they do will succeed.

4 *But wicked people are not like that.*
They are like chaff that the wind blows away.
5 *So the wicked will not escape God's punishment.*
Sinners will not worship with God's people.
6 *This is because the LORD takes care of his people,*
but the wicked will be destroyed. (NCV)

? Ask questions that will help you interact with the passage.

The most **A**ssuring verse(s): V. 6 – "...the Lord takes care of his people..."

How would I say the verse in my own words or language?
The Lord watches over those whose lives please him, so they are always assured of his protection and care.

What does this verse mean for me? How will I live and think differently because of this verse?
If I am living a godly life, I can be confident that God will watch over my life and my future. I need to live for him rather than for my own desires!

My most **B**eloved verse(s): *V. 2 – "They love the Lord's teachings, and they think about those teachings day and night."*

How should I say the verse in my own words or language?
Those who find great joy and satisfaction in God's word spend time thinking about his word all of the time.

What does this verse mean for me? How will I live and think differently because of this verse?
It means having an inner joy for God's word which will happen only when I make a habit of thinking about it throughout the day, whenever I can. Honestly, I haven't been thinking much about God's word. I've been so busy lately that I haven't taken time to remember his promises and instructions. Lord, I pray that you'll give me a greater desire to read and think deeply on your

word day and night!

The most **C**onvicting verse(s): *V. 1 – The part about "don't listen to the wicked, don't go where sinners go..."*

How would I say the verse in my own words or language?
Those who do not follow the advice of sinful people, or hang out with people who influence them away from the Lord or who mock God, will live joyful and happy lives.

What does this verse mean for me? How will I live and think differently because of this verse?
I've been hanging out with a friend who always wants me to get drunk with him. I've told him I don't want to do that anymore, because the Bible tells me not to get drunk or lose my self-control. But he doesn't respect my values and beliefs, so he continues to pressure me to get drunk. After reading this verse, I'm convinced that I need to avoid those situations and to stop spending time with him.

Example of FLY Method

📖 **R**ead John 10:27-30

"My sheep listen to my voice; I know them, and they follow me.

I give them eternal life, and they shall never perish; no one will snatch them out of my hand. My Father, who has given them to me, is greater than all; no one can snatch them out of my Father's hand. I and the Father are one." (NIV)

? **A**sk questions that will help you interact with the passage.

Focus on two verses (I've chosen verses 27 & 29, and copied the verses in my notebook.):

V. 27 – My sheep listen to my voice; I know them, and they follow me. They shall never perish; no one will snatch them out of my hand.

V. 29 – no one can snatch them out of my Father's hand.

Look up the meaning of unfamiliar words.
[Notice that I underlined words that are unfamiliar to me. I then look up the meanings of unfamiliar words in my dictionary.]

Meanings: Sheep symbolize those who are believers. The sheep follow where the shepherd will lead them. They listen to the shepherd's voice.

Snatch - to take something quickly: to grab or grasp somebody or something hastily.

Perish - to die, disappear: to come to an end or cease to exist.

Listen.

What I am hearing from you, Lord, is that you are the shepherd and I am your sheep. You take good care of me. I am safe and secure in you. No one can take me away from you! How reassuring this is! No matter what happens to me, I will still belong to you.

Your response: *Father, you are good. I praise you that I have eternal life because of what Jesus has done for me! Thank you that you know me. Thank you that Jesus will really take care of me because he is my Shepherd. Help me to listen to you and follow you with my whole heart. Thank you for these new truths you taught me today!*

Example of PURE Method

📖 **R**ead Luke 10:38-42

"As Jesus and the disciples continued on their way to Jerusalem, they came to a certain village where a woman named Martha welcomed him into her home. Her sister, Mary, sat at the Lord's feet, listening to what he taught. But Martha was distracted by the big dinner she was preparing. She came to Jesus and said, 'Lord, doesn't it seem unfair to you that my sister just sits here while I do all the work? Tell her to come and help me.' But the Lord said to her, 'My dear Martha, you are worried and upset over all these details! There is only one thing worth being

concerned about. Mary has discovered it, and it will not be taken away from her.'"

? Ask questions that will help you interact with the passage.

Pick: *The character I've picked is Martha.*

Uncover: *I heard Jesus is coming through my town. I'm excited! Jesus and his disciples usually visit us since they are good friends with my brother Lazarus and my sister Mary and me. We always look forward to having him at our home. So now they're here and I have not finished cooking! Jesus looks tired and hungry. But as soon as they were seated on the floor Jesus started to teach! I went back to the kitchen, and I wish Mary would come and help me. But there she is at Jesus' feet, so attentive to what he is saying. Does she not realize I need help? I'm upset that she's leaving me with all this work here. Does Jesus not even notice? In my frustration, I went to Jesus and said, "Lord, doesn't it seem unfair to you that my sister just sits there while I do all the work? Tell her to come and help me." But instead of doing that, he lovingly reminded me what my priorities should have been. He said, "My dear Martha, you are worried and upset over all these* details! There is only one thing worth being concerned about. Mary has discovered it, and it will not be taken away from her." I felt embarrassed. I realized the truth of his words. I am so busy and worried about this meal that I forgot that I need to feed my hungry soul as well. Now I admire my sister for choosing the latter. I missed all the "spiritual food" this day because my priorities were not in order.

Relate: Like Martha, I get too busy with my job, household chores, my children's activities, church activities, and other good things. I've been serving Jesus, but spending time with him has not been my priority. What Jesus told Martha about being worried and upset over things that won't last made an impression on me. It's like he is directly talking to me!

Express: Lord, thank you for reminding me to set my priorities right, to spend time with you first thing every day before doing anything else.

Example of PICTURES Method

📖 Read Proverbs 11:12-31

? **A**sk questions that will help you interact with the passage. Is there a...

Promise I can hold on? *I love the* <u>*promise*</u> *in v. 25: "The generous will prosper; those who refresh others will themselves be refreshed."*

Instruction I should obey? *V. 24: "Give freely and become more wealthy; be stingy and lose everything." Forgive me, Lord, for not being generous toward poor people and toward your work. I want to be an obedient child of yours, so please help me to give more freely.*

Challenge to face? *I find v. 16* <u>*challenging*</u>*! "Without wise leadership, a nation falls; there is safety in having many advisers." I tend to keep my problems and troubles to myself. It's not easy for me to ask for advice or counsel from my mature Christian friends. Lord, please give me the courage to talk to my friend about this problem that has been bothering me for a while.*

Truth about God that's new to me: *V. 20: "The LORD detests people with crooked hearts, but he delights in those with integrity." God knows my heart and my every thought. Thank you, Lord, for reminding me of* *this truth today. Check my heart and my thoughts that I may live a clean life before you.*

Unanswered question I should find out? *I don't quite understand v. 30. What does "the tree of life" refer to?*

Rebuke I should heed? *V. 28: "Trust in your money and down you go!" Wow, I really should pay attention! I know I have a tendency to trust in my money! Lord, please don't allow this to happen to me. May I live a godly life. Thank you for this timely rebuke, Lord!*

Encouraging word? *V. 16: "A gracious woman gains respect...." I've been told that I'm kindhearted and gracious. Thank you Lord for the respect I'm getting from my friends and family. What an encouragement!*

Sin to confess? *V. 13: "A gossip goes around telling secrets...." Lord, I confess the sin of gossip. Please forgive me! Give me the discipline to keep my mouth shut about things I shouldn't tell my friends! I realize I don't want people to gossip about me, either!*

Appendix B

To Whom Should We Pray?

The Bible says there is only one God, but that he exists in three persons. We describe this with terms like Three-in-One, Holy Trinity, or Triune God. It is impossible for us to fully understand this with our limited human minds. But it does mean that we can address our prayers to God the Father, God the Son (Jesus), or God the Holy Spirit, because God is one.

Jesus taught his disciples to pray to the Father. For example, in Matthew 6:9 he says, *"This, then, is how you should pray: 'Our Father in heaven...'"* (NIV). We are to pray to the Father in the name of Jesus, because Jesus is our mediator who gives us access to the Father (1 Timothy 2:5). He said *"No one can come to the Father except through me"* (John 14:6).

However, he also said we can pray to him (that is, Jesus). See John 14:14, *"ask me for anything in my name."* In John 15:15, he said, *"I have called you friends, for everything that I learned from my Father I have made known to you"* (NIV). Since Jesus calls you his friend, you can talk to him as friend to friend. What an amazing privilege!

The Bible doesn't directly tell us to pray to the Holy Spirit, but when we pray to God we know that God in his entirety hears us. We are told that the Holy Spirit participates in our prayers, helping us when we don't know how we should pray (Romans 8:26-27).

To whom should we NOT pray? We should never pray to other gods (Psalm 115:3-8; Isaiah 45:20), for the Bible tells us there is only one true God (Isaiah 37:20; 1 Timothy 1:17; Jude 1:25). Also, the Bible does not teach us to pray to angels, and we are told to not worship them (Colossians 2:18; Revelation 22:8-9). We should not pray to our ancestors or other people who have died, for God says we must not try to communicate with the spirits of the dead (Deuteronomy 18:10-12). Instead, we are told to trust and rely on God alone (Psalm 24:3-4; Psalm 40:4). He is the only one to whom we should pray.

Appendix C

Finding a Church

It is very important that you have fellowship with other Christians. If you take a red hot coal from a fire and set it by itself, what happens to it? It quickly grows cold and black, while the other coals remain hot. In the same way, we need each other! God has made us for community. He has given all of us different gifts, so that together we can bless each other and fulfill his purposes. A hand that is not attached to the body can't accomplish much! (See 1 Corinthians 12:12-27.) We all need to be taught, encouraged, prayed for, corrected, and helped in many ways.

However, finding a good church is not always easy. You might live in a country with few Christians, or where it is perhaps even illegal to talk about Jesus. So how can you find Christian fellowship?

The first thing you must do is PRAY. Ask the Lord to lead you to true, godly followers of Christ; people who love Jesus, who believe the Bible, and who teach it correctly. Ask him to help you recognize what is true and what is false, because there are false Christians, false teachers, false prophets, and false churches. The Bible warns us many times to watch out for them (Matthew 7:15 & 24:24; 1 Timothy 1:3; 2 Peter 2:1, etc.).

A true church must proclaim Jesus Christ as Lord (1 Corinthians 8:6 & 12:3; 1 John 2:22-23), and acknowledge that he is God in the flesh (John 1:1-18; Romans 8:3; 1 John 4:1-3). It must also teach that we can be saved by no other name than that of Jesus (John 14:6; Acts 4:12), because he is the one who died for our sins, was buried, and was raised from the dead (1 Corinthians 15:3-4). There are other signs that can indicate whether a church is true or false, but the first question to ask is, "What do they say about Jesus?"

Do you already have a friend or relative in your country who is a follower of Christ? They can probably help you find a church. The people who introduced you to Jesus may also be able to help you, even if they are in another country.

Some English-speaking churches can be found at www.internationalchurches.net. (Most of those churches probably include services and Bible studies in the national language as well.) If there is no church where you live, you might be able to find a Bible study group to join. Even if you can only meet with one other Christian for prayer, Bible study, and mutual encouragement, do it! Jesus said, *"For where two or three gather together as my followers, I am there among them"* (Matthew 18:20).

Finding a Bible

If you don't own a Bible, you might be wondering how to get one. There are several possibilities.

If you know a church or another Christian, they can probably provide you with a Bible or tell you where you can buy one. You might be able to find them in bookstores. Some countries even have stores that specialize in Bibles and Christian books. Also, unless the websites are blocked in your country, you should be able to order a Bible from the Internet. You can order Bibles in several languages from sites like www.biblica.com, www.christianbook.com, www.bibles.com, and others (perhaps even a website in your own language).

You can read the Bible online. One excellent site, www.biblegateway.com, allows you to read and compare Bible translations in many different languages. It's very useful when you want to search for a certain verse, word, or subject in the Bible.

Many people like to use Bible apps on their smartphones or tablets. This way they almost always have a Bible with them. Three excellent, free, multilingual Bible apps are *YouVersion Bible App*, Olive Tree's *The Bible Study App*, and *Bible Gateway*.

Although apps and online Bibles are useful and convenient, you will also want to own a physical Bible. A book still works when batteries die, or when websites are blocked or hacked.

Old Testament/New Testament: The Bible has two main sections called the Old Testament (OT) and New Testament (NT). The OT is the part that was written before Jesus entered the world just over 2,000 years ago. The NT is the part written shortly after his life on earth.

Sometimes the NT is printed separately because that way it is smaller and less expensive, yet it still communicates the most important things we need to know about God. However, both the OT and NT are the word of God, and we need to read the OT to properly understand the NT. So when you are buying a Bible you should be aware that if it says "New Testament", it is only that.

In many countries Christians are persecuted, oppressed, or restricted. If this is true in your country, then it might be difficult for you to find a Bible. If you do have one, you will need to be wise and cautious. As Jesus told his disciples, *"I am sending you out like sheep among wolves. So be as wise as snakes and as harmless as doves"* (Matthew 10:16, NIrV®).

Questions? Comments?

I hope this book is helpful for you as you learn the habit of spending Quiet Time with the Lord "morning by morning". If you have questions or comments, we would love to hear from you. You can contact us at isiportland@isionline.org.

Acknowledgments

My first clear teaching about Quiet Time came at an InterVarsity Christian Fellowship training camp in the Philippines, where staff taught, modeled, and emphasized Quiet Time as a part of daily life. I am grateful to them, and also to those mentors whom I have not met but whose books have had a big influence on me in this area, including Don Whitney, Brother Lawrence, Catherine Marshall, Evelyn Christenson, Dick Eastman, and others.

I am thankful to many friends who prayed, kept me accountable, and encouraged me along the way. My special appreciation to Dr. Miriam Adeney for looking at the manuscript and making several helpful suggestions.

I want to acknowledge my son BJ, from whom I borrowed a couple of key word ideas, and my daughter Jolleen, for her idea to use icons to identify steps more easily. Along with my daughter-in-law, Cheryl, they have prayed with me through the writing of this book. I thank God for each one of them.

I am most thankful to my loving and patient husband, Kerry, who spent many long hours proofreading and editing the manuscript, as well as writing Appendices B and C. I am very blessed to have him in my life.

Above all I thank the Lord Jesus for giving me the exciting task of writing this book. What a joy to share with you what I have learned from him. I give him all the glory!

JQS

15113523R00065

Made in the USA
San Bernardino, CA
15 September 2014